THE TRAINER'S POCKETBOOK

D0772166

By John Townsend
Illustrations by Phil Hailstone

"The most creatively practical book on the subject. Even the most experienced trainer will find a handful of ideas."
Management Centre Europe, Brussels

"The Trainer's Pocketbook is an extremely useful collection of helpful hints, suggestions and reminders for trainers and presenters. It is standard handout material for all instructors we train."
Richard Franklin, Education Program Manager, Hewlett-Packard, France

First published in 1985 by Thamesman as The Instructor's Pocketbook.
All subsequent editions published by Management Pocketbooks Limited,
14 East Street, Alresford, Hants SO24 9EE UK

US edition published jointly by Management Pocketbooks Limited and
Stylus Publishing, LLC, 22883 Quicksilver Drive, Sterling, VA 20166

Seventh edition   The Instructor's Pocketbook 1994
Eighth edition   as The Trainer's Pocketbook 1996 (Reprinted 1997, 1998)
Eighth edition (US)   1999

Printed and bound in USA by Sentinel Press Printing Co., Inc., St. Cloud, MN.

ISBN: 1-57922-020-7

CONTENTS

INTRODUCTION

INTRODUCTION

Training is a valued and rewarding profession because it is dedicated to helping people grow. A Master Trainer's performance can be measured on 3 dimensions:

Knowledge and Experience

● Technical competence in subject matter(s) taught ● Practical 'on the job' experience
● Academic qualifications ● Knowledge of the training function
● Competence in promoting training

Trainer Skills (Design and delivery of Training Courses)

● Training needs analysis ● Applying learning theory to course design ● Keeping trainer recall high ● Making learning fun ● Performing (voice control, eye contact, body language, etc) ● Developing and using audio-visual support
● Leading discussions ● Creating and conducting exercises ● Training evaluation

Concern and Availability

● Empathy ● Listening skills ● Asking and answering questions ● Dealing with 'difficult' trainees ● Facilitating ● Adapting style/content to fit trainees' needs

3D TRAINER GRID

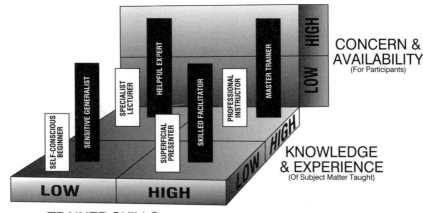

© John Townsend and Paul Donovan, 1994

**Beware
of the Expert!**

A 'Has-Been'

A 'Drip under pressure'

LEARNING THEORY

LEARNING THEORY

BRAINS
HOW ADULTS LEARN

- If they want and need to
- By linking learning to past, present or future experience
- By practicing what they have been taught
- With help and guidance
- In an informal and non-threatening environment

BRAINS

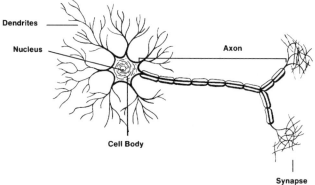

Neurologists are now saying that the average brain contains
100 billion brain cells (neurons). Each one is like a tiny tree with messages passing from
branches to roots, each making hundreds of connections to other cells as we think. The
total 'megabyte' capacity is inconceivably large.

BRAINS

DO BRAINS DECLINE?

The myth that brain power declines with age has finally been exploded.

- If the brain is stimulated **no matter at what age** new 'twigs' will grow on each brain cell's branches and increase the total number of possible connections

- Some of the world's most creative people have been exceptionally prolific at advanced ages (Gauguin, Michelangelo, Haydn, Picasso)

- We generate new brain connections more rapidly than the average loss of brain cells - even if we lose 10,000 brain cells a day from birth, the total number lost at age 80 would be less than 3%

LEARNING THEORY

BRAINS
SPEED/PREFERENCES

Neurologists have a lot to teach teachers and trainers! Recent experiments in Brussels have shown that:

- The average person can think at 800 words per minute but the average trainer can only talk at 120 wpm - **so we must give our participants something interesting to do with their spare 680 wpm!**

- The brain goes into 'auto shut-off' after only 10 minutes if it is not given something to stimulate it - **so we must vary the media and give multi-channel messages!**

- When a message is given once, the brain remembers 10% one year later; when it is given six times, recall rises to 90% - **so we must repeat, recap and review**

- The brain prefers: rounded diagrams and figures to square ones; Times and Helvetica typefaces; dark letters on light background; color, color, color!!!

BRAINS

RETENTION: THE PROOF

It may be that our brains retain every piece of information they ever receive:

- **Death-type experiences:** people snatched from death say that their entire life flashed before them

- **Hypnosis:** under competent supervision hypnotees have unlocked vast memory banks

- **Surprise stimulation:** the 'déja vu' experience may be triggered by sights, sounds or smells

- **Experiments:** in experiments where patients received electrode treatment, they 're-lived' past, forgotten experiences

- **Mnemonics:** using special 'memory systems' normal people can rival famous stage magicians

LEARNING THEORY

BRAINS

RECALL: 5 MAIN FACTORS

FIRST
We are more likely to remember the beginning of events or the first in a series of events

REVIEWED
Recall falls rapidly after 24 hours without review

OUTSTANDING
We remember unusual things exceedingly well!

LINKED
Recall is high for things which are linked by mnemonics or analogy

LAST
We are more likely to remember the end of events or the last in a series of events

The Finnish **FROLL**
(A cousin of the Norwegian Troll)

(11)

BRAINS
RECALL OVER TIME

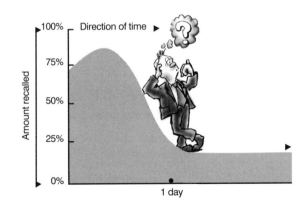

LEARNING THEORY

BRAINS
HOW TO KEEP RECALL HIGH

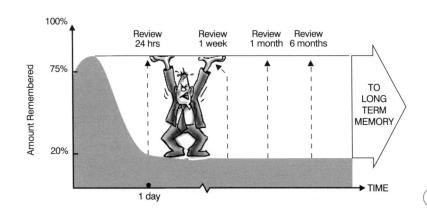

(13)

BRAINS

BRAINS - LEFT AND RIGHT

Logical

- Speech
- Calculations
- Intellectual Analysis
- Reading
- Writing
- Naming
- Ordering
- Sequencing
- Complex motor sequences
- Critique
- Evaluation
- Logic

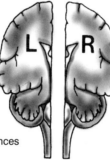

c**R**eative

- Creativity (new combinations)
- Artistic activity
- Musical ability/Rhythm
- Emotions
- Recognition
- Comprehension
- Perception of abstract patterns
- Spatial abilities
- Facial expressions
- Holistic ability
- Intuition
- Images
- Color

(14)

BRAINS

STIMULATING THE LEFT AND RIGHT BRAIN

Professional trainers encourage learners to use both sides of the brain. Experiments have shown that:

- People who have been trained to use one side of the brain more than the other (accountants, engineers, versus artists, musicians) find it difficult to 'switch' when necessary

- When the weaker side is stimulated and encouraged to co-operate with the stronger side there is a greater synergy (1 + 1 = 5!)

Example: Newton understood the theory of gravity while day-dreaming

Applications: Trainers should combine analytical exercises with creative, expressive activities

BRAINS

VHF

To help trainees use both sides of the brain we must remember that information is stored with **V**ery **H**igh **F**requency - in VHF!

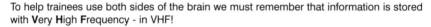

VISUAL
• Pictures • Scenes • Images • Logos • Diagrams • Graphs
• Charts • Photos • Drawings

HEARING
• Words • Music • Sounds • Accents
• Conversations

FEELING
• Emotions • Smells • Tastes
• Tactile experiments • Pain/Comfort

An ongoing classroom experiment I've been conducting over the last few years shows that, when tested after 24 hours, participants' recall of a **V** message (80% correct answers) and an **F** message (79% correct answers) is almost twice as good as their recall of an **H** message (45% correct answers).

BRAINS

MULTI-CHANNEL MESSAGES

Because people can store information in the left **and** the right brain in the form of pictures (**V**), words (**H**) or sensations and feelings (**F**) we, as professional trainers, must give **multi-channel messages.**

This means giving colorful visual back up to our verbal messages at the same time as appealing to trainees' emotions and senses.

These messages will be stored simultaneously in several parts of the left and right brain and therefore multiply the chances of recall.

(17)

BRAINS

MNEMONICS

Many devices exist to help people recall multi-channel messages. The Germans call them 'donkey bridges' (Eselsbrücke) because they help the donkey of ignorance across the bridge to knowledge! They are **mnemonics** (memory devices) which **link together** two or more pieces of information. By linking together visual, hearing and/or feeling data, the donkey bridge creates a distinct and more memorable whole.
Example: the FROLL on page 11!

Note: A mnemonic (not newmonic!) is from a Greek word and means **any** kind of memory device, not just first letter acronyms.

Interestingly, neurologists report that donkey bridges actually do provide a link across the brain's **real** bridge between the right and left brain (the corpus collosum)!

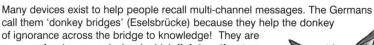

BRAINS

DONKEY BRIDGES

Here are 5 kinds of donkey bridges which trainers can use to revolutionize trainee recall!

- **First Letter Acronym** (Flac!)
  Take the first letter of every word or phrase to be remembered and create a new word and (if possible) image
  Example: As a trainer you should **pamper** the audience with your voice by using pampers - **P**rojection **A**rticulation **M**odulation **P**ronunciation **E**nunciation **R**epetition **S**peed (see page 53)

- **First Letter Phrase** (Flep!)
  Create a phrase where each word begins with the letter of each thing to be remembered in a list
  Example: **R**ichard **O**f **Y**ork **G**ave **B**attle **I**n **V**ain
  to remember the colour sequence of **R**ed **O**range **Y**ellow **G**reen **B**lue **I**ndigo and **V**iolet in a rainbow

BRAINS

DONKEY BRIDGES

- **Sounds**
  Select music, songs or sound effects which will remind your
  trainees of your messages when they hear them in the future
  Examples: Use a polka (POLCA) as the theme tune for a management
  course on **P**lanning **O**rganizing **L**eading **C**ontrolling **A**chieving;
  Tina Turner's 'You're The Best' for a sales team course

- **Rhymes & Slogans**
  Create a memorable rhyme or slogan to 'anchor' your training message
  Examples: For a trainer it's 'Optional to be a professional'; Peace Corps
  water-saving slogan for the Caribbean: 'When it's yellow let it
  mellow, when it's brown, flush it down!'

- **Logos and Image Association** (Lima!)
  Design a logo for your course; create visual aids which help
  trainees remember key messages by associating them with
  a powerful picture - logos last longer!
  Example: Think of any flag or any company logo and reflect on
  all the messages this simple shape brings to your mind

LEARNING THEORY

MIND SET

However hard we try to keep trainee recall high, the enemy is **Mind Set**. When people hear or see something that clashes with their beliefs or values, they experience **Cognitive Dissonance**. Because of the discomfort caused by this dissonance, they will either justify their present beliefs/behavior or distort the new information so that it no longer challenges their 'world view'. Some famous people have been victims of their mind set!

- 'Who the hell wants to hear actors talk?' (Harry Warner, 1927)

- 'There is no likelihood that man can ever tap the power of the atom' (Robert Millikan, Nobel Prize, 1923)

- 'Sensible and responsible women do not want to vote' (Grover Cleveland, 1927)

- 'Heavier-than-air flying machines are impossible' (Lord Kelvin, 1895)

MIND SET

Faced with inevitable and totally natural problems of mind set, we trainers must help our trainees to overcome the discomfort caused by cognitive dissonance. Like Shakespeare's Mark Antony, we must start from **their** point of view ('Brutus was an honourable man') and find a **WIIFT** (**W**hat's **I**n **I**t **F**or **T**hem?) to help them change their minds.

By concentrating on **WIIFT**s we help them to justify changing their skills, knowledge or attitudes by providing a real need to do so.

Example: Faced with a salesperson whose mind set is 'I should be out selling, not listening to this nonsense', you should concentrate on how your course can help her sell more.

Exercises:

- Think of one of your own courses. What WIIFTs can you think of for a 'dinosaur' trainee whose mind set is 'our present system has worked very well up to now'?

- How could you find WIIFTs to overcome the following mind set:
  'What can this upstart teach **me**; s/he's half my age!"?

LEARNING ENVIRONMENT

THE IDEAL ENVIRONMENT
CHECKLIST

- Good audio visual equipment (see appropriate section)
- Appropriate seating patterns (pp 25-30)
- Comfortable chairs
- Good writing surface for each participant
- Thermostatically controlled temperature (ideal ambient temperature = 65° F)
- Independently controlled ventilation (air conditioning or windows)
- Good supply of coffee/light lunches
- Adequately sound-proofed room, with 15-20 square feet space per participant
- Natural daylight (windows with blinds/curtains)
- Central electrical commands (lights, audio visual, etc)

LEARNING ENVIRONMENT

SEATING PATTERNS

1. 'U' shape

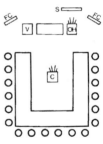

Advantages
- Businesslike
- Trainer can walk into 'U'
- Generally good participant visibility
- Standard, therefore non-threatening

Disadvantages
- Somewhat formal; needs ice-breaking
- Some participants masked by audio visual equipment
- Front participants constantly at 60-90° (neck ache)
- Rear participants are far from screen/flip chart

FC = Flip Chart / OH = Overhead / S = Screen / C = Carousel / V = Video

SEATING PATTERNS

2. 'V' shape

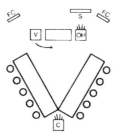

Advantages
- Best pattern for visibility/neck ache
- Optimum trainer/participant contact
- Less formal and intimidating than 'U'

Disadvantages
- Space requirements (only small groups)

FC = Flip Chart / OH = Overhead / S = Screen / C = Carousel / V = Video

SEATING PATTERNS

3. Herring Bone

Advantages
- Space effective for large numbers
- All participants at good angle to screen/flip chart, etc
- Trainer can walk down 'spine'

Disadvantages
- Several participants hidden by others
- Reminiscent of school
- Encourages dysfunctional groupings
- Rear participants far from screen/flip chart, etc
- Relatively poor participant/trainer contact

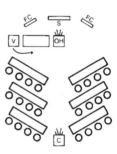

FC = Flip Chart / OH = Overhead / S = Screen / C = Carousel / V = Video

SEATING PATTERNS

4. 'Bistro'

Advantages

- Ideal for 'teambuilding' sessions and small group workshops
- Informal: encourages maximum trainee participation/identification
- Original: encourages open-mindedness
- Trainer can 'circulate'

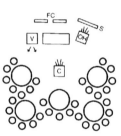

Disadvantages

- Some participants have poor visibility or may be constantly at an angle to screen/flip chart
- May foster lack of attention and encourage side conversations
- Encourages splinter group identification

FC = Flip Chart / OH = Overhead / S = Screen / C = Carousel / V = Video

SEATING PATTERNS

5. Circle

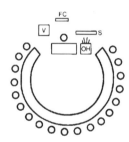

Advantages

- Ideal for sensitivity training sessions
- Encourages maximum participant involvement
- Excellent trainer/participant contact
- Minimum side conversations;
  no informal group formation

Disadvantages

- Difficult to find tables which can be set up in a circle
- Some participants have poor visibility/neck ache
- Without suitable tables participants may feel unnecessarily 'exposed'
- Overtones of 'touchy/feely' style encounter groups

FC = Flip Chart / OH = Overhead / S = Screen / C = Carousel / V = Video

SEATING PATTERNS

6. Amphitheater

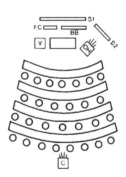

Advantages

- If room is well designed, excellent visibility and acoustics
- Very space-effective
- Good for lecture-type presentations

Disadvantages

- Very poor trainer/participant contact
- Difficult to set up unless room is designed with permanent seating
- Back rows must be elevated
- Very university-like

 FC = Flip Chart / OH = Overhead / S = Screen / C = Carousel / V = Video

SEATING PATTERNS

PSYCHOLOGY

- Research shows that distance reduces participation - trainees in back rows are less likely to participate than those in front

- Any kind of 'row' reduces interaction: it is difficult for those in the back row to hear front row contributions and for those in the front row to twist round to interact with people behind

- Changes in seating patterns from one session to another can be psychologically upsetting for participants

- At repetitive sessions participants will invariably sit in the same place

- Angry or cynical participants will attempt to move away from a group seating pattern

LEARNING ENVIRONMENT

SETTING UP THE ROOM

MEDIA

VARYING THE MEDIA

As a general rule the learning environment should provide a change of pace/medium/subject/blood circulatory pattern every 10 minutes to avoid 'auto shut-off' (see page 9).

The professional trainer will, therefore, plan seminar coverage so that new audio-visual interventions, and new topics, come at fairly regular 10 minute intervals.

S/he will also plan for regular discussion periods, small group work or 'stretch breaks' to fight the descending learning curve.

Lastly, voice control (pitch, volume, modulation) can help change the pace of a seminar.

(34)

PREPARING TO TRAIN

THE 5 W'S

QUESTIONS TO ASK

The success of a seminar, course or instructional module depends on a great number of variables. Before preparing yourself to train, you must answer 5 questions specifically - the 5 **W**'s!

WHY?
- Ask why you are training at all. What are the trainees' objectives? What should trainees think or do at the end of the course?

WHAT?
- Ask what you can put over in the available time. At what intellectual level will you pitch your teaching? What audio visual aids will you need?

WHO?
- Analyse the trainee group: Age? Nationality? Level? Language abilities? Prior experience? Expectations? Mind set?

WHEN?
- Ask whether the timing of the course is good for you and for them. Period of year? Weekdays/weekends? Morning? Afternoon? Evening?

WHERE?
- Ask about and prepare for environment. Building? Room? Layout? Seating patterns? Interruptions? Temperature? Noise?

STRUCTURE

HOW TO DESIGN A LEARNING EXPERIENCE

B. GUNAR EDEG R.A.F. (B) *
The Icelandic pilot who joined the Royal Air Force
('B' Squadron)

* This mnemonic device will help you remember the
  14 vital steps in designing a well-structured and
  memorable learning experience.

STRUCTURE

DESIGN: STEP 1

B ANG
- Always start with a learning 'hook' or attention-getter

G AP
- Establish the gap between participants' present skills/knowledge and those to be acquired during the course

U NDERSTAND
- Check that participants understand the existence and size of skills/knowledge gap

N EED
- Establish the need for participants to close the skills/knowledge gap

A SK/ANSWER
- Ask and answer questions to check participants' individual needs (encourage those with smaller gap/need to help with 'teaching')

R OUTE MAP
- Outline course coverage, stressing results to be achieved (during and after the course) in closing skills/knowledge gap

STRUCTURE

DESIGN: STEP 2

E**xplain**

D**emonstrate**

E**xercise**

G**uide/correct**

- Explain each new skill/learning in digestible chunks using appropriate **V**isual, **H**earing and **F**eeling support (see page 80)

- Demonstrate skills and/or show how knowledge applies to them; use **VHF** support

- Allow participants to exercise each new skill or to feedback their understanding of new knowledge

- Show participants how well they have learned and correct any inadequacies

STRUCTURE
DESIGN: STEP 3

$\boldsymbol{R}_{ECAP}$

$\boldsymbol{A}_{CTION\ PLAN}$

$\boldsymbol{F}_{OLLOW\text{-}UP}$

$\boldsymbol{B}_{ANG}$

- Review all learning points at end of each module (or beginning of next); use **VHF** support

- Agree on an action plan for the transfer of new skills or knowledge to real life

- Agree on any follow-up or refresher

- Always finish with a succinct and provocative encapsulation of the learning experience

MEMORY TECHNIQUES

NAME CARDS

Unless you are in a formal school setting, make sure that each participant is provided with a ready-made or do-it-yourself 'tent card' for his/her name. Ask for big bold letters so you can read the name from any part of the teaching area.

Tip With cardboard tent cards, bend over a corner to keep the card from collapsing.

COURSE TIMING

DOWN TIME

In a training day of 9 hours (8.30 a.m - 5.30 p.m) always plan for down time as follows:

- Latecomers, settling, housekeeping = 10 mins

- Coffee/Tea breaks = 20 + 20 = 40 mins
  (even if you have planned 15 minute breaks!)

- Lunch and 're-settling' after lunch = 75 mins
  (even if you have planned 1 hour!)

- Stretch breaks, breaking into small groups
  and other miscellaneous
  down time = 25 mins

  Total = 2 hrs 30 mins

COURSE TIMING

TIMING TIPS

- Always keep a clock or watch on your desk - but don't rely on looking at the watch on your wrist

- Use an alarm clock or good kitchen timer for timing break-out sessions, separate modules, etc

- Always allow time for discussion - build it in to your course plan

TRAINING METHODS

EFFECTIVENESS OF DIFFERENT METHODS

Ranking of methods depending on TEACHING GOALS (1 = high, 8 = low)

METHOD	KNOWLEDGE ACQUISITION	ATTITUDE CHANGE	PROBLEM-SOLVING SKILLS	INTER-PERSONAL SKILLS	PARTICIPANT ACCEPTANCE	KNOWLEDGE RETENTION
CASE STUDY	4	5	1	5	1	4
WORKSHOP	1	3	4	4	5	2
LECTURE	8	7	7	8	7	3
GAMES	5	4	2	3	2	7
FILMS	6	6	8	6	4	5
PROGRAMMED INSTR.	3	8	6	7	8	1
ROLE-PLAYING	2	2	3	1	3	6
'T' GROUP	7	1	5	2	6	8

Source J. Newstrom *Evaluating Effectiveness of Training Methods*

TRAINER PREPARATION

HOW TO BEAT MURPHY!

- Always carry a checklist of material, equipment, etc, to the training site

- Arrive at the training site at least one hour before the start of the program to prepare material and equipment

- Take at least 15 minutes from this time to prepare yourself:
  - physically; centering energy, grooming, posture and breathing
  - mentally; visualizing the participant group, trying to imagine how they are feeling and asking/answering the question, 'How can I best **help** these people to change and grow, given the program objectives and organizational culture?'

TRAINER PREPARATION

PERSONAL STANDARDS

- Consciously manage personal energy levels by avoiding temptations to over-eat, over-drink or under-sleep before or during the program

- Keep physically fit with at least one type of exercise per week

TRAINING DELIVERY

PREPARING TO TEACH

NAMES AND FACES

When faced with a room full of new trainees you will need to remember their names

- Listen to name
- Spell it in your head
- Repeat name as often as possible during training event
- Look for an outstanding facial feature
- Exaggerate the feature
- Associate

Mrs Hawkes	=	beaked nose
Mr White	=	sickness/fear/clown
Mr Metropoulos	=	big town, city slicker

This will ensure you can address
(and impress) them during coffee
break, lunch, etc.

TRAINING DELIVERY

ICEBREAKERS

Professional trainers always start with an **Icebreaker** or **Inclusion Activity** (see page 110 for some examples).

WHY?

- When trainees arrive in a training room they are usually a loose mix of individuals with different mind sets

- At the beginning of a course, trainees are usually **not** thinking about the trainer or the course content but about their neighbor; coffee time for phoning/messages; the end of the day for errands; sights, sounds and smells in the room, etc

- An inclusion activity will make them feel **included** and, if well designed, help them to relate to the others in the group; it can also provide a bridge into the course itself

- Above all it puts the spotlight on **them** (the most important people in the room) and takes if off **you** and allows you to relax into the course

ICEBREAKERS

WHAT? A good inclusion activity should be:

Foolproof: has been tested and works!

Amusing: trainees should enjoy it

Bridged: linked to the course subject (if possible)

Unique: trainees should not have done it before

Lively: has movement, exchange and chatter

Optimistic: is positive and non-threatening

Uncomplicated: is easy to explain and organize

Short: lasts between 5 and 10 minutes

This donkey bridge was developed by
Richard Hamilton and the 'Red Team' at
the WWF Train the Trainer Course, April 1994.

50

ENTHUSIASM

YOU GOTTA BELIEVE!

- If you're not enthusiastic about your subject, how can you expect the trainees to be!!

- Consciously use your eyes and eyebrows to communicate enthusiasm

- Always keep a sparkle in your voice

- Fight boredom of repetitive sessions by introducing new anecdotes, examples, etc, or by changing lesson structure

BANG!

NERVES: THE MURPHY MONKEY

As you get up to speak, it's as if a monkey has suddenly jumped onto your shoulders. He claws at your neck and weighs you down - making your knees feel weak and shaky. As you start to speak, he pulls at your vocal chords and dries up your saliva. He pushes your eyes to the floor, makes your arms feel 10 feet long and attaches a bungee to your belt - pulling you back to the table or wall behind you! Experienced speakers know about the Murphy monkey. Within the first 30 seconds they throw him to the audience! When you throw the monkey to one of the participants, suddenly the spotlight is on them and not on you. How ...?

- A question, a show of hands, a short 'icebreaker' (participant introductions, an exercise or quiz, etc) a discussion, a 'volunteer' or simply a reference to one or more of the participants - all these are ways of putting the monkey on **their** backs for a few moments

    This takes the pressure off you and gives you time to relax, smile and get ready to communicate your message loud and clear.

USING YOUR VOICE

PROJECTION   Speak louder than usual; throw your voice to back of room

ARTICULATION   Don't swallow words
Beware of verbal 'tics'

MODULATION   Vary tone and pitch; be dramatic, confidential and/or triumphant

PRONUNCIATION   Check difficult words
Beware of malapropisms

ENUNCIATION   Over emphasize
Accentuate syllables

REPETITION   Repeat key phrases with different vocal emphasis

SPEED   Use delivery speed to manipulate the audience; **fast** delivery
to excite and stimulate; **slow** delivery to emphasize,
awe, dramatize and control

(53)

YOU CAN'T NOT COMMUNICATE

Research has shown that when someone gives a spoken message the listener's understanding and judgement of that message come from:

7% WORDS

- Words are only labels and listeners put their own interpretation on speakers' words

38% PARALINGUISTICS

- The **way** in which something is said (ie: accent, tone, inflection, etc) is very important to a listener's understanding

55% FACIAL EXPRESSIONS

- What a speaker looks like while delivering a message affects the listener's understanding most

- Research source - Albert Mehrabian

MANNERISMS

- Don't be tempted by manual props (pens, pointers, spectacles, etc)
- Don't keep loose change in your pocket
- Be aware of your verbal tics and work on eliminating them (ie: 'OK!' - 'You know' - 'and so forth' - 'Now ...')
- Watch out for furniture!
- Avoid 'closed' or tense body positions
- Don't worry about pacing, leaning, etc
- Check your hair/tie/trousers/dress before standing up!

DRESS

- Avoid black and white and other strongly contrasting colors

- Wear comfortable, loose-fitting clothes

- If you can't make up your mind, wear something boring - at least your clothes won't detract from the message!

- Try and dress one step above the audience

- Check zippers and buttons before standing up

Tip for Men   When in doubt, a blue blazer, grey pants and black shoes with a white shirt and striped tie are usually acceptable from the board room to the art studio.

LIGHTHOUSE TECHNIQUE

Sweep the audience with your eyes,
staying only 2-3 seconds on
each person - unless in dialogue.

This will give each participant the impression
that you are speaking to him/her personally
and ensure attention, in the same way as
the lighthouse keeps you awake by its
regular sweeping flash of light.
Above all, avoid looking at one
(friendly-looking) member of the
audience or at a fixed (non-threatening)
point on the wall or floor.

FACILITATING DISCUSSION

QUESTIONING SKILLS

| **Closed Questions** | - | 'Who can tell me on which date?' |
| | - | 'Which/what specifically?' |

Open Questions
- 'About'   - 'How do you feel about ...?'
- Reflective   - 'You don't feel comfortable with ...?'
- Hypothetical - 'What do you think would happen if ...?'
- Framing   - 'Help me to see how this fits with ...?'
- Silence   - ....?
- Statements   - 'Rosemary, you look as if you wanted to say something'

Always avoid: Multiple - a string of questions

Leading   - 'Don't you think it would be better to ...?'

FACILITATING DISCUSSION
LUBRICATORS

Verbal
- 'I see'
- 'Ah, ah'
- 'That's interesting!'
- 'Really?'
- 'Go on!'
- 'Tell me more about that'

Non-Verbal
- Nodding
- Constant eye contact
- Leaning forward
- Stepping aside
- Raising eyebrows
- Frowning (encourages clarification)

(59)

FACILITATING DISCUSSION
REFLECT/DEFLECT

Most participant questions are not questions. They are requests for the spotlight. If it's one of those rare, closed **real** questions - answer it succinctly. If not, first:

- **REFLECT** back to the questioner what you thought was the question ('If I understand correctly, you're asking ...')

Depending on how the questioner 'reformulates' the question, answer it, **OR**

- **DEFLECT** it as follows:

  - **Group** : 'How do the rest of the group feel?'
    : 'Has anyone else had a similar problem?'

  - **Ricochet** : (to one participant) 'Bill, you're an expert on this?'

  - **Reverse** : (back to questioner) 'You've obviously done some thinking on this. What's **your** view?'

FACILITATING DISCUSSION
ACTIVE LISTENING

Whenever a participant interrupts or responds emotionally during a course s/he is probably overstating his or her feelings in order to justify the 'outburst'. In **every** such case use Active Listening. Never attempt to counter, argue, defend or take sides.

1. Take the outburst as a positive contribution (smile, encourage, nod)
2. Successively reflect back to the participant (in the form of questions) what feelings you heard being expressed. 'You're upset with ...?' 'You're unhappy about ...?' 'You feel that we should ...?' Active listening has 3 advantages:

   ● You show the participant you're interested and not defensive
   ● You allow the participant to confirm that what you heard was what s/he meant **or** to correct your interpretation
   ● You quickly lead the participant to specify the **exact** problem and to suggest a solution

TRAINING DELIVERY

FACILITATING DISCUSSION
'B'ING

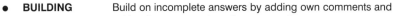

Here are 4 ways to keep a group discussion going:

- **BUILDING**   Build on incomplete answers by adding own comments and asking for agreement or disagreement

- **BOOSTING**   Support timid participants' contributions, boost their confidence and ask for extra comment

- **BLOCKING**   Interrupt dominant/talkative/aggressive participants by asking what others think

- **BANTERING**   Establish non-threatening atmosphere by engaging in friendly repartee with responsive participants

FACILITATING DISCUSSION

BRAINSTORMING

A technique for obtaining ideas from a group. Here's how:

Ask Ask for/provoke ideas; if necessary wait 45 seconds before giving own

Record Write **all** ideas on a flip chart (number them for future reference) - don't evaluate until end

Trigger Use 'B'ing discussion techniques to encourage participants to trigger ideas

Summarize Summarize and/or regroup ideas; help group to choose best

FACILITATING DISCUSSION
SOCRATIC DIRECTION

Take a tip from the Ancient Greeks.

If you wish to encourage audience participation to prove a point use **Socratic Direction.**

Know the answers you want

Use open questions

Paraphrase participants' answers

Summarize contributions (on a flip chart?)

Add your own points

FACILITATING DISCUSSION

TEACHING TEMPO

Two factors will govern the tempo of your material coverage and discussion periods:

1. The participants' level of knowledge and general intelligence
    - low = slow
    - high = fast

2. Your own teaching style
    - snappy/authoritarian/directive = fast
    - relaxed, informal, facilitative = slow

How to change tempo

- Slower - Use more cases, examples, anecdotes; speak slower;
  ask open questions

- Faster - Speak faster; use more directive tone; cut down discussions;
  ask closed questions

DEALING WITH DIFFICULT PARTICIPANTS

1. The Heckler

- Probably insecure
- Gets satisfaction from needling
- Aggressive and argumentative

What to do:

- Never get upset
- Find merit, express agreement, move on
- Wait for a mis-statement of fact and then throw it out to the group for correction

DEALING WITH DIFFICULT PARTICIPANTS

2. The Talker/Know All

- An 'eager beaver'/chatterbox
- A show-off
- Well-informed and anxious to show it

What to do:

- Wait until he/she takes a breath, thank, refocus and move on
- Slow him/her down with a tough question
- Jump in and ask for group to comment

DEALING WITH DIFFICULT PARTICIPANTS

3. The Complainer

- Feels 'hard done by'
- Probably has a pet 'peeve'
- Will use you as scapegoat

What to do:

- Get him/her to be specific
- Show that the purpose of your presentation is to be positive and constructive
- Use peer pressure

DEALING WITH DIFFICULT PARTICIPANTS

4. **The Whisperers** (There's only one; the other is the 'whisperee'!)

- Don't understand what's going on (clarify or translate)
- Share anecdotes triggered by your presentation
- Are bored, mischievous or hypercritical (unusual)

What to do:

- Stop talking, wait for them to look up and 'non-verbally' ask for their permission to continue
- Use 'lighthouse' technique (see page 57)

DEALING WITH DIFFICULT PARTICIPANTS

5. The Silent One

- Timid, insecure, shy
- Bored, indifferent

What to do:

- Timid?   Ask easy questions; boost his/her ego in discussing answer; refer to by name when giving examples; bolster confidence
- Bored?   Ask tough questions; refer to by name as someone who 'surely knows that ...'; use as helper in exercises

DEALING WITH DIFFICULT PARTICIPANTS

PSYCHOLOGICAL JUDO
(when classical methods have not worked!)

In physical judo you use the energy of your opponent to cause his downfall by changing your 'push' into 'pull'. In psychological judo you ask the difficult participants to be **even more** difficult. This gives them even more of the spotlight and attention than they wanted and they will use their energy to 'pull back' to avoid ridicule or overkill.

Classical Confrontation

Psychological Judo

* See page 73 for examples

(71)

DEALING WITH DIFFICULT PARTICIPANTS
PSYCHOLOGICAL JUDO

Example:

The Joker

These are the participants that need the spotlight and constantly play to the crowd by chipping in with more or less humorous remarks or put-downs of you or other participants. Sometimes they try and entertain their neighbors with asides, winks, grins and nudges.

Instead of trying to discipline them and alienate a potentially useful participant, why not attempt to channel the humorous energy for everybody's benefit?

The psychological judo solution would consist of asking them to use their joker's talent to help the group. For example, you could ask them to take notes in order to present a humorous monologue or parody of the learning at the end of each day.

(72)

DEALING WITH DIFFICULT PARTICIPANTS
PSYCHOLOGICAL JUDO

Examples:

1	The Heckler	Appoint as class 'devil's advocate'. Insist that s/he criticizes **whenever** s/he feels you are leading class astray. Demand negative remarks.
2	The Know-All	Agree with and amplify 'know-all' contributions. Ask for expert judgement when none is forthcoming. Get him/her up front to teach short module. Refer constantly to their expertize in subject matter taught.
3	The Complainer	Ask for written list of objections to help class maintain sense of realism. Get him/her to read list at end of day. Add to list whenever possible!
4	The Whisperers	State that time is short and ask those who don't understand not to interrupt but to ask their neighbor!
5	The Silent One	State that some people are shy and dare not participate. This does not mean they have not understood. Encourage shy ones not to participate.

TYPES OF BODY LANGUAGE

POSTURES & GESTURES

- How do you use hand gestures? Sitting position? Stance?

EYE CONTACT

- How's your 'Lighthouse'?

ORIENTATION

- How do you position yourself in class?

PROXIMITY

- How close do you sit/stand to participants?

LOOKS/APPEARANCE

- Are looks/appearance/dress important?

EXPRESSIONS OF EMOTION

- Are you using facial expressions to express emotion?

POSTURES AND GESTURES: HANDS

STEEPLING

- Self Confidence (Intellectual Arrogance)

HAND CLASP

- Anxious, controlled

NOSE TOUCH

- Doubt

'L' CHIN REST

- Critical evaluation

MOUTH BLOCK

- Resisting speech

POSTURES AND GESTURES: SITTING

ARMS UP
- Reserved, defensive

ARM/LEG CROSS
- Closed, unconvinced

LEAN FORWARD
- Ready!

LEAN BACK
- Confident superiority

LINT-PICKING
- Disapproval

POSTURES AND GESTURES: STANDING

THUMBS OUT

- In charge! Dominant

FIG LEAF

- Self-control, tense

ARMS OUT

- Open, sincere, conciliatory

TABLE LEAN

- Authoritative, involved

LEAN ON

- Unthreatened, casual belongingness

TRAINING DELIVERY

TEN TIPS

- Don't keep your eyes on your notes
- Never read anything except quotations
- If you're not nervous there's something wrong
- Exaggerate body movements and verbal emphasis
- **Perform** (don't act); perform = 'fournir' (to supply) and 'per' (for)
- Pause often - silence is much longer for **you** than for the audience
- Use humor; a laugh is worth a thousand frowns!
- Be enthusiastic; if you're not, why should they be?
- Don't try and win the Nobel prize for technical accuracy
- **KIS** - **K**eep **I**t **S**imple!

Audio visual support

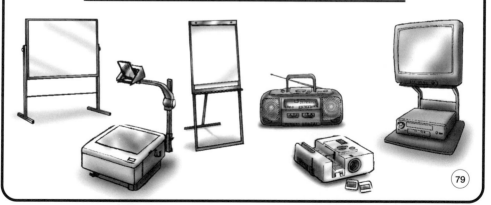

VHF COMMUNICATION

The human brain stores information in **VHF** - as **V**isual, **H**earing or **F**eeling data (see page 16).

Each trainee has a preferred channel for remembering data. In my on-going classroom experiment on trainee recall, 52% of participants say that their memory favors visual information; while only 7% prefer words/lectures and sounds. An astonishing 41% say they remember feelings, tastes, smells and tactile experiences best.

In order to 'tune in' to the maximum number of trainees' wavelengths, professional trainers use a wide range of transmitters!

V
- Flip chart • Bulletin Board • Whiteboard • OHP • Slide Projector
- Props and Accessories • Video clips • Word pictures • Imaging

H
- Music (instant access CD's or Minidiscs for changes of mood/illustrations)
- Sound effects • Audio gimmicks • Onomatopoeia

F
- Music (emotion/mood setting) • Handouts • Verbal descriptions • Anecdotes
- Metaphors • Parables

Feelings stay longer than facts!

AUDIO VISUAL SUPPORT

PRESENTATION KIT

MASKING TAPE

TIMER

THICK COLORED MARKERS

SCISSORS

SPARE TRANSPARENCIES AND OVERHEAD PENS

(81)

FLIP TIPS

PREPARATION

INVISIBLE OUTLINE

Lightly pencil in headings in advance when unsure of space, drawing, handwriting, etc

CORNER CRIB

Use the top corner to pencil in your notes for each chart. Write small and no one will notice!

READY-MADE

Prepare key charts in advance

FLIP TIPS

PAPER

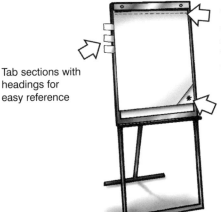

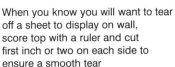

When you know you will want to tear off a sheet to display on wall, score top with a ruler and cut first inch or two on each side to ensure a smooth tear

Tab sections with headings for easy reference

Cut corners off preceding sheets when you need quick access to a particular page

AUDIO VISUAL SUPPORT

FLIP TIPS

GRAPHICS

ATTRACTIVE

- Give each flip a title
- Use bullet points (like the ones on this page)
- Use at least 2 dark colors

BIG & BOLD

- Use **thick** markers (bring your own!)
- Should be legible from 30 feet!

CAPITAL KEYWORDS

- Never write sentences!

FLIP TIPS

GRAPHICS

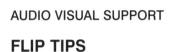

Whenever possible use **cartoons** or **drawings** to dramatize and add interest to your headings.

85

AUDIO VISUAL SUPPORT

FLIP TIPS

GRAPHICS

Standing

Every time you turn your back on the audience your voice and their attention disappear.

Since you can't write **and** face the audience at the same time (unless you are a contortionist!) you should:

- Write (a few words/seconds)
- Turn and Talk
- Write (a few words/seconds)
- Turn and Talk

AUDIO VISUAL SUPPORT

THE WHITEBOARD

WRITING AND STICKING

Write on!
- Replaces blackboard (school memories)
- Great for brainstorming (see page 63)
- Change color often
- Only use appropriate whiteboard pens

Stick up!
- Use 3M 'Post-it' stickers to create group-work summaries (key phrases only); stick on whiteboard
- Move stickers into columns or categories; use pens to draw bubbles round salient groupings or to make links between stickers

BULLETIN BOARD

The lightweight, collapsible bulletin board is the ideal visual aid for facilitators and project leaders.

Writing	Cover bulletin board surface with large sheet of brown paper. Use as flip chart.
Pinning	Distribute colored cards for exercises/group work. Collect and pin to board in categories. Add headings, illustrations, etc.
Sticking	Cover board with large sheet, spray with contact glue. Stick cards/cut outs as above.

TEXT TIP

AUDIO VISUAL SUPPORT

OVERHEAD PROJECTOR RULES

THE PROJECTOR

- Make sure the projector lens and projection surface are clean before starting your presentation (if you can't get hold of some glass cleaning liquid and a cloth, turn the projector off and use a handkerchief)

- Check for a spare projector lamp

- Test projector/screen distance with a sample transparency for positioning and focus

OVERHEAD PROJECTOR RULES

PROJECTION ANGLE

- How to avoid the 'Keystone' effect

AVOIDING THE "KEYSTONE" EFFECT

Keep the projector beam at 90° to the
screen by tilting the screen (ideal) or by
jacking up the projector until keystone
disappears; if you jack the projector you'll
need something to prevent transparencies sliding forward

PROJECTOR POSITIONING

AUDIO VISUAL SUPPORT

OVERHEAD TIPS
PLANNING A PRESENTATION

Use the 'Storyboard' approach

- One transparency with **chapter headings**
- One transparency **per** chapter heading
- One transparency per point/topic in each chapter
- Use consistent design (see p 93)
- Print series name and number on each
- Concentrate message in center
- Use only $2/3$ of space for message

AUDIO VISUAL SUPPORT

OVERHEAD TIPS

GOLDEN RULES

F_{RAME} Use a standard **horizontal** frame with your 'Logo' for all transparencies

L_{ARGE} **Use large, legible letters**
Titles = ½" - ¾"   Text = ¼" - ½"

I_{MAGES} Use illustrations on all transparencies
Words are not visual aids!

C_{OLOR} Use 2-3 complementary colors on **all** transparencies

K_{IS} Keep it simple
One idea only per transparency
- Maximum 6 lines of text
- Maximum 6 words per line

OVERHEAD TIPS
PRODUCING TRANSPARENCIES

- Laser print computer-generated visuals directly onto a transparency

- Cut and paste original artwork and text, then photocopy onto a transparency

- Write/draw directly onto a transparency (with permanent or non-permanent pens)

AUDIO VISUAL SUPPORT

OVERHEAD TIPS
PRODUCING TRANSPARENCIES

Freehand Lettering

- Use permanent overhead pens
- Place transparency on squared paper to ensure alignment
- Use color as much as possible
- Be bold! Practise your own 'alphabet'
- For solid letters, use light color to block in letters before outlining with darker color

AUDIO VISUAL SUPPORT

OVERHEAD TIPS

PRODUCING TRANSPARENCIES

Symbols

- Wherever possible
  use symbols as
  well as letters

AUDIO VISUAL SUPPORT

OVERHEAD TIPS

PRESENTATION TECHNIQUES

Overlay

- Use several superimposed transparencies to build up a story or argument
  Note: Make sure you mount your overlays so that they fit onto each other
  exactly - everytime

With Plastic Frame (Staedtler)

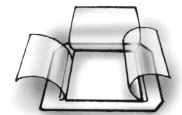

With Card Frame (3M)

AUDIO VISUAL SUPPORT

OVERHEAD TIPS
PRESENTATION TECHNIQUES

Revelation

- When you have several important
  points on one transparency,
  use a mask to reveal your
  argument step by step
  (if you don't, your audience
  will be reading point 6 when
  you're talking about point 1)

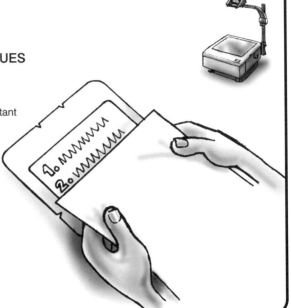

AUDIO VISUAL SUPPORT

OVERHEAD TIPS
PRESENTATION TECHNIQUES

- Use a **Pointer** to highlight messages

  eg: use cut out arrow, transparent
  pointing finger, pen or pencil
  (be careful it doesn't roll off)
  or a laser pointer

- Place pointer on the
  transparency and move as
  you change messages;
  Don't hold it; Murphy says
  your hand will shake!

POINTERS

- Position your pointer here first

- Next move it here

PRESENTATION TECHNIQUES

(99)

AUDIO VISUAL SUPPORT

OVERHEAD TIPS
USING THE PROJECTOR

P*REPARE*
- Prepare transparencies in sleeves; in the right order; unclipped

P*LACE*
- Place a transparency on the projector; align; switch on

P*OSITION*
- Do not block any participant's view of the screen; switch off projector between each transparency

AUDIO VISUAL SUPPORT

THE LCD PANEL

An LCD panel placed on a powerful (minimum 400 watt) overhead projector allows you to display your laptop presentation on the normal classroom projector screen.

- Colorful, professional
- 'Multimedia' animation possible
- Pre-determined sequence of visuals
- No messy acetate storage problems

- Often over-complicated/confusing graphics
- Technically subject to Murphy's Law!
- Easy to forget that words and figures are not visuals!
- Definition of graphics not always as crisp as transparencies

(101)

AUDIO VISUAL SUPPORT

MUSIC

Here are some ways you should be using recorded music in your training seminars:

- To create a friendly atmosphere at the beginning of the course as participants come in, meet each other and settle down

- As background music during coffee breaks/intervals

- To provide a relaxed 'learning' environment during exercises, tests, etc

- As an introductory 'bang'

- To create specific atmospheres for special messages (film music, theme tunes, sound effects, etc)

- To illustrate a point amusingly with a song 'snippet' (example for a course on Customer Service: 'Help', 'Keep the customer satisfied', 'You can't always get what you want', etc)

THE CD/MINIDISC PLAYER
VOICE

Recorded speech can be useful for:

- Illustrating role-plays (Interviewing, Public Speaking, Salesman-Customer, Boss-Subordinate)

- Examples of opinions (market research interviews, etc)

- Bringing an absent colleague to the seminar

- Interjecting humorous anecdotes

- Giving examples of current radio ads/trends

- Use a cassette deck to record your presentation so you can work on your mistakes

Note When recording audio examples make sure you leave very little space between each recording. In this way you can press the 'pause' button at the end of one example knowing that the next recording is cued to start as soon as you next hit the button.

PHOTOGRAPHIC SLIDES

WHEN TO USE PHOTOGRAPHIC SLIDES

- When you have the time and the money!
- When you need a 'higher quality' presentation
- When you want to show photographs/cartoons, etc
- When you wish to change pace or differentiate from colleagues' omnipresent overhead slides
- When you wish to dramatize a point and create expectancy by darkening the conference room
- When contact with and participation of the audience are not essential

PHOTOGRAPHIC SLIDES

WHEN NOT TO USE PHOTOGRAPHIC SLIDES

- When you only have words to show
- When you can't darken the room sufficiently
- When audience participation is important
- When you are a persuasive 'eye contact' speaker
- When you have a tight budget!
- When 'everybody else does, so I suppose ...'
- When you don't know how to work the projector

VIDEO AND CD-i

In today's multi-media world, video and CD-i are virtually indispensable tools for professional trainers. Here are some advantages and disadvantages of the medium:

- Professional, fast-moving
- In tune with trainees' background/expectations
- Can be adapted to LCD panels/video projection when monitor not available/too cumbersome

- Few videos give **exactly** the message you want
- Expensive to buy/hire
- Technically subject to Murphy's law

TIPS

- Edit your own video clips at home (2 VCRs needed)
- Use only snippets which support your message

(106)

AUDIO VISUAL SUPPORT

MURPHY'S LAW

'If something can go wrong - it will!'

O'Connor's corollary:
'Murphy was an optimist!'

- The only way to beat Murphy is to be a professional and use the 3 P's:

  • **Preparation**   • **Preparation**   • **Preparation**

GROUP & INDIVIDUAL EXERCISES

GROUP & INDIVIDUAL EXERCISES

ICEBREAKERS

Here are **3** ideas for 'inclusion activities' (see pages 49 & 50) to supplement the classic 'please introduce yourself/your neighbor' presentations.

- **2 True, one False**
  Participants introduce themselves by giving one incorrect and two correct pieces of information about their background; likes and dislikes; present job, etc - the group must guess which is true and which false

- **Famous Pairs**
  Write the names of some famous pairs on post-its (Romeo/Juliet, Laurel/Hardy, etc) and stick them at random on participants' backs so they can't see who they are; they must then locate their 'partner' by asking others questions about their identity - these questions may only be answered by Yes or No

- **Stick-up Needs**
  Ask each participant to write 1-3 objectives for attending the course on separate post-its/cards and to stick them on a flip chart or pinboard while explaining to the others; alternatively, you can collect the cards and stick them up - asking for comments as you do so

THE QUIZ

In training courses where facts must be learned it is essential to 'exercise' participants' new knowledge. Written tests are fine but remind people of their school days.

A well-devised quiz will appeal and test at the same time.

Suggestions

- Break group into quiz teams to provoke competition
- Invent different categories of questions (like TV game shows)
- Keep scores on imaginatively designed board (whiteboard/bulletin board)
- Don't forget the prizes!

GROUP & INDIVIDUAL EXERCISES

CASE STUDIES

Case Studies

Concisely written, practical and realistic case studies will induce thinking, analysis, pro and con discussion and genuine efforts to find solutions to problems. Case studies help participants to apply theoretical knowledge to real-life situations and also serve as 'pace-changers' to stimulate interest and attention.

Case Study Rules for Trainers

- Know the facts of case study well
- Have pre-prepared questions to guide trainees during their own analysis of the facts
- Tabulate consensus items during discussion
- Encourage differences of opinion to explore alternative solutions
- The trainer should use Socratic Direction (see page 64) to summarize learning points from the case study

GROUP & INDIVIDUAL EXERCISES

VIDEO RECORDING

Nowadays video cameras are idiot and almost Murphy-proof! Recording trainees in individual or group practice sessions is a very powerful teaching tool!

TIPS

- Use a camcorder so you can rewind and play back without moving the tape
- Prepare connections to the TV monitor in advance to avoid delay
- Use fast forward during playback to save time
- If you have the equipment, record separate individuals/groups on different tapes and split into sub groups for playback

People are hyper-sensitive about seeing themselves on video
First reactions of trainees who are not used to the medium concern their **hairstyle**, their **weight** and their **accent**
Even when they accept their **look** and **sound** they may over- react with self-criticism and become depressed or defensive

Always accept these reactions with sympathy and sensitivity, and stress confidentiality. Use professional feedback technique (see page 115)

GROUP & INDIVIDUAL EXERCISES

ROLE-PLAYING 1

Role-playing

Role-playing is a dramatized form of case study in which trainees act out a human relations problem under the guidance of the trainer who elicits an evaluation of the performance in light of previously taught principles.

Pre-requisites for a successful role-playing exercise:

- The role play situation must be realistic
- The situation must be one with which participants can identify; characters should be of a type that really exists in the organization
- Participants must live their parts
- Role-playing should not represent a threat to timid participants
- Trainer should play the 'challenger' role

Role-playing is not play acting. It is 'reality practice'.

ROLE-PLAYING FEEDBACK RULES

1. First ask role-player(s) for a 'self-critique'
2. Ask group to take notes and watch the video re-play (where appropriate)
3. Ask the group to give feedback

Rules

- Always separate 'motivational' from 'developmental' feedback

- For developmental feedback, use the conditional tense and always offer an alternative (ie: 'I think it would have been more effective if you had ...')

- Always address the individual concerned and say 'you' not 'he/she'

GROUP & INDIVIDUAL EXERCISES

PROJECT WORK

Projects

In modular courses and seminars, given at regular intervals, (weekly, monthly, etc) project work between sessions provides an ideal bridging, learning and review experience.

1. **Tailor-made** As a trainer you should develop relevant project structures which will allow trainees to practice each session's learning points - if possible in groups of 4-7

2. **Canned** Many video-based packages exist which provide inter-session project work as an integral part of the course

PROJECT WORK

THE GROUP RECAP

One kind of project worth highlighting is the group recap.

In courses which last more than one day, split the group into small teams and ask a different team to make a summary of the previous day's learning at the start of each new day.

Teams invariably vie with one another to make **their** summary the best (at least the most amusing), a lot of learning takes place and a good time is had by all (especially the trainer who has one less module to present!).

GROUP & INDIVIDUAL EXERCISES

INSTRUMENTS

Seminar Instruments

3 examples of instruments which can be used to develop or sustain interest, provide a point, gather information, etc.

● **Matrix**	● **Grid/Window**	● **Questionnaire**

Matrix

FACTORS OR CRITERIA	/////////
1	
2	
3	
4	
5	

- Decision-making
- Behavioral Analysis
- Plotting of variables (ie: who does what to whom)

Grid/Window

HI X

LOW

　　HI　　LOW

- To plot a combination of 2 characteristics

Questionnaire

1 _____
2 _____
3 _____
4 _____
5 _____
6 _____
7 _____

- Self-awareness
- Attitude survey
- Polling facts

FURTHER READING AND VIEWING

Learning

'Preparing Instructional Objectives' by Robert Mager, Kogan Page, 1990

'Superlearning' by Ostrander & Schroeder, Sphere, 1992

'The Adult Learner - a neglected species' by Malcolm Knowles, Gulf, 1990

'Learning to Listen, Learning to Teach' by Jane Vella, Jossey-Bass, 1994

'Accelerated Learning' and *'Music to Learn By'* from author Roger Swartz, Essential Medical Information Systems, Box 1607, Durant, OK 74702-1607, USA

'The Learner's Pocketbook' by Paul Hayden, Management Pocketbooks, 1995

General

'Techniques of Training' by Leslie Rae, Ashgate, 1995

'Training Costs Analysis' by Glenn E Heard, ASTD, 1994

'Improving Trainer Effectiveness' edited by Roger Bennett, Ashgate, 1988

'Instructor Excellence' by Bob Powers, Jossey-Bass, 1992

'Active Training' by Mel Silberman, Jossey-Bass, 1997

'The In-House Trainer as Consultant' by Holdaway & Saunders, Kogan Page/Stylus Publishing, second edition, 1996

FURTHER READING AND VIEWING

General (continued)

'A Handbook for Training Strategy' by Martyn Sloman, Ashgate, 1994

'Facilitating' by Mike Robson, Ashgate, 1995

'Influencing with Integrity (NLP)' by Genie Laborde, Syntony, 1987

'Graphics for Presenters' from author Lynn Kearney, Crisp Publications

Video: *'Ten Training Tips',* John Townsend, Melrose Film Productions, 1994

Brains and Memory

'Your Memory - a User's Guide' by Allan Baddeley, Trafalgar Square, 1994

*'The Mind Map Book: How to Use Radiant Thinking to Maximize Your Brain's
  Untapped Potential'* by Tony Buzan, Plume, 1996

'Mind and Brain' from Scientific American, September 1992

Mindpower (video tapes) by Tony Buzan, BBC, 1991

'Brain Mind', monthly, edited by Marilyn Ferguson, Box 42211, Los Angeles, CA 90042, USA

Video: *'Memories are Made of this',* John Townsend, Melrose Film Productions, 1994

THE MANAGEMENT POCKETBOOK SERIES

**New US editions co-published
with Stylus Publishing ($8.95 each)**
Business Presenter's Pocketbook
Facilitator's Pocketbook
Manager's Pocketbook
Teamworking Pocketbook
Time Management Pocketbook
Trainer's Pocketbook

**Also now available in the US
($8.95 each)**
Appraisals Pocketbook
Assertiveness Pocketbook
Business Planning Pocketbook
Business Writing Pocketbook
Challengers Pocketbook
Coaching Pocketbook

Communicator's Pocketbook
Creative Manager's Pocketbook
Customer Service Pocketbook
Empowerment Pocketbook
Interviewer's Pocketbook
Key Account Manager's Pocketbook
Learner's Pocketbook
Managing Change Pocketbook
Managing Your Appraisal Pocketbook
Manager's Training Pocketbook
Marketing Pocketbook
Meetings Pocketbook
Mentoring Pocketbook
Motivation Pocketbook
Negotiator's Pocketbook
People Manager's Pocketbook
Performance Management Pocketbook

Project Management Pocketbook
Quality Pocketbook
Sales Excellence Pocketbook
Salesperson's Pocketbook
Self-managed Development Pocketbook
Stress Pocketbook
Telesales Pocketbook
Thinker's Pocketbook
Trainer Standards Pocketbook

**Pocketfiles (for description, see
next page - $39.95 each)**
Trainer's Blue Pocketfile of
Ready-to-use Exercises
Trainer's Green Pocketfile of
Ready-to-use Exercises
Trainer's Red Pocketfile of
Ready-to-use Exercises

About the Author

John Townsend, BA MA MIPD
John is Managing Director of the Master Trainer Institute.
He founded the Institute after 30 years of experience in
international consulting and human resource management
positions in the UK, France, the United States and Switzerland.

From 1978-1984 he was European Director of Executive
Development with GTE in Geneva with training responsibility
for over 800 managers in some 15 countries. Mr Townsend
has published a number of management and professional
guides and regularly contributes articles to leading management
and training journals.

In addition to training trainers, he is also a regular speaker at conferences and leadership
seminars throughout Europe.

Contact
John Townsend, The Master Trainer Institute,
L'Avant Centre, 13 chemin du Levant, Ferney-Voltaire, France
Tel: (33) 450 42 84 16   Fax: (33) 450 40 57 37
E-mail: john.townsend@wanadoo.fr

ORDER FORM

Call toll free, fax, mail or e-mail today!
Stylus Publishing, LLC PO Box 605, Herndon, VA 20172-0605
Tel: 703 661 1581/800 232 0223 Fax: 703 661 1501 E-mail: Styluspub@aol.com
Please prepay in US dollars. We accept American Express, MasterCard and Visa. Checks payable to "Stylus Publishing."

Name/Attn _____

Title _____

Company _____

Address _____

_____ City _____

State _____ Zip/Postal Code _____

Country _____

I enclose payment by (check box):
Check ☐ American Express ☐ Visa ☐ MasterCard ☐

Card No. ☐☐☐☐☐☐☐☐☐☐☐☐☐☐☐☐

Expiry Date _____/_____/_____

Signature _____

Day time tel. _____

Please send me the following title/s:

	Price	Qty	Total Cost
_____	____	____	____
_____	____	____	____
_____	____	____	____
_____	____	____	____
VA residents add 4.5% sales tax			____

Please send complete Corporate Training catalog ☐

Add shipping Surface mail: US Canada & Mexico, $3.75 1st copy; $0.75 each additional _____

[Source Code: MPBK]

Total payment $ _____